a life together

a life together

*Wisdom of Community from
the Christian East*

BISHOP SERAPHIM SIGRIST

PARACLETE PRESS
BREWSTER, MASSACHUSETTS

A Life Together: Wisdom of Community from the Christian East

2011 First Printing

Copyright © 2011 Bishop Seraphim Sigrist

ISBN: 978-1-55725-800-7

Scripture references marked KJV are from the Authorized King James Version of the Holy Bible.

Scripture references marked RSV are from the Revised Standard Version of the Bible, copyright © 1946, 1952, and 1971 by the Division of Christian Education of the National Council of the Churches of Christ in the United States of America. Used by permission. All rights reserved.

Library of Congress Cataloging-in-Publication Data

Sigrist, Seraphim.
  A life together : wisdom of community from the Christian East / by Seraphim Sigrist.
      p. cm.
  Includes bibliographical references.
  ISBN 978-1-55725-800-7
  1. Church—Meditations. 2. Communities—Religious aspects—Christianity—Meditations. I. Title.
  BV600.3.S55 20110
  262'.019--dc22

                                        2010051153

10 9 8 7 6 5 4 3 2 1

Published by Paraclete Press
Brewster, Massachusetts
www.paracletepress.com
Printed in the United States of America

Contents

preface

To discover the church is to discover community.

This can be disquieting and unexpected for a new Christian. So C. S. Lewis's diabolical tempter Screwtape writes that "when he gets to his pew and looks around him he sees just that selection of his neighbors whom he has hitherto avoided." From this can come the more or less unconscious feeling that "he is showing great humility and condescension in going to church with these 'smug' commonplace neighbors at all."

Of course, as Screwtape notes, this feeling involves the subconscious illusions that these neighbors are insignificant in God's eyes, and also that somehow since they are not wearing togas they are not of the same family as the Christians of the New Testament time were.

Community entered into in this illusory way—as mere church activity, or as judgment—will at most create segmentation of one's life: hearty and perfunctory greetings on Sunday and perhaps an occasional committee meeting or parish outing. So then a faith that began so brightly becomes but the spiritual compartment of a life with many other compartments scarcely related to it at all.

The systematic effort to destroy religious faith that was so central to the communist regime in Russia was many sided. It included the closing of churches, the harassment of believers, the inculcation of atheism through the schools, and also one more insidious dimension that was beyond the possibility or imagination of the Roman persecutor in the days of the early martyrs—the limitation of church activity, in those churches allowed to remain open for the time, to the formal and ritualistic. No meetings to study and discuss the Bible. No Sunday schools. No prayer circles. Not even the tea or coffee after liturgy or the parish picnic, which are the sort of minimums of the American church community.

In this the enemies of Christianity showed a realization like that of Screwtape's—that in attacking the possibility of community, they strike at the core of what Christianity is. Yet, as again and again before in history when the church is attacked or in decline, it manifests a power of resurrection. As the Russian priest, and leader of Christian renewal, Fr. Alexander Men said:

> Christianity is the religion of death, instantly transformed into life. . . . "They counted us as dead, but lo we are alive." These words spoken by the Apostle Paul have resonated for all time. Throughout the Church's history there were incredible disappointments and it often seemed that she was crushed, but by the power of God she resurrected as many times . . .

Fr. Men said this in response to a question at an impromptu meeting around a table in a home where people had gathered to meet him. These meetings were themselves a resurrection of that principle of community that the enemies of faith had so assiduously sought to destroy.

Mark Weiner, who had been baptized by Fr. Men, was one of those who made his home available for these dangerous but vital meetings and he summarizes the situation of the time well:

From the beginning of the 1980s, the KGB pressures on Fr. Men's parish in Novoderevnya intensified. Frequently he was called in for interrogation and warnings. There were interrogations and arrests of parishioners. Even the briefest opportunities for meeting with his spiritual children in the tiny office of the pastor, in the little house by the church, were forbidden. Thus the talks about Christ, the church, the Bible, and life and death moved to private homes and kitchens.

The form of the parish's infrastructure was the "gatherings." This is how we referred to the groups of Fr. Men's parishioners (mostly young people) who met weekly in private homes for communal prayer, for Bible study, and for the "union of all." Gathering was the name chosen by Father deliberately so that the criminal words "group" or "seminar" would not suddenly leak out by accident (especially over tapped phones). For the KGB these words constituted a ready criminal charge. These "gatherings" were in fact the usual means of meeting with Fr. Alexander outside the church.

But the word *gathering*, when you think of it, is the most basic translation of the original word for "church," *ecclesia*, isn't it? Driven by necessity and with the visionary leadership of a priest, a most basic and precious reality of the church was recovered in kitchens and living rooms of Moscow homes. For the Lord said, in words definitive of the church, "Where two or three are gathered together in my name there am I in the midst of them," and also, "If two or three of you shall agree on any thing and they shall ask it, it shall be done."

This coming together in agreement is at the beginning at Pentecost, isn't it? "When the day of Pentecost was fully come, they were all with one accord in one place"—a return to the accord of Pentecost in the new terms and situation of the church in our time. It was Fr. Men's conviction that the historical church was just at the beginning of its way. "The Church is in its infancy," he liked to say: just beginning to open out the possibilities of Pentecost.

This recovery of community is something that has happened, and is happening still, in many places. The recovery happened in Russia under persecution, and happens today within the new freedom there and in many other places in the Christian world. We need only mention the meeting of the pope with hundreds of thousands from the "new communities" gathered in Rome to realize something of the scope of this movement.

For me personally, however, it is the village of Semkhoz, a small town in the woodland north of Moscow that expresses most fully the experience of Christian community. There Fr. Men had his home and there he was assassinated in 1990 as, one could say, a last martyr of the time of persecution.

In 1995 I was asked to speak to a group of mostly young people about the spiritual inheritance of Fr. Men and the house meetings that marked his ministry. The talk was held in his own home. I remember it as a bright day of the special sort of clarity in the air that one feels perhaps once or twice in a year. Walking in the woods I felt a particular presence of Pentecost in the cool and luminous air, having met gathered community that day.

Not much in that talk about community, as far as it goes, would I change. I say "as far as it goes" because I would wish to go further, but before addressing that possibility let us look at what I said there in the house in Semkhoz. I said that community is the agreement of persons like that of the disciples at Pentecost. That within this agreement each person receives the gift of his or her self. As Trappist monk Thomas Merton said, "From now on, brother, each man stands on his own feet." Merton's use of the word *brother* locates this gift as within community.

What I would go on to say is this:

> Now, if the gift of ourselves and the ability to stand on our own feet is a first discovery in community, I would add a second discovery and gift found in community: Our continuing agreement to share life together opens out into a deeper and deeper oneness with the others of our community. We live into a friendship in the full sense that Jesus spoke of when he said, "From now on I call you friends."

> Community is an ongoing entering into friendship, for the mystery of community is that of friends, and the giving of our lives for our friends. This friendship is the ongoing gift of the ever deeper realization of

the law of sharing and exchange, living Jesus' command to "bear one another's burdens."

The friends who have given their lives to each other in the Lord, these are the two or three who agree, these are the disciples gathered with one accord at Pentecost.

I said then, and would say the same now, that the gifts of the Holy Spirit are revealed in community. As such, they are for all the community, and so one gift does not quench the other, even when, as happens often, they are opposite. So the analytical does not quench the emotional, the gift of tears does not quench that of laughter, the gift of the spiritual elder does not contradict that of the psychologist, the gift of ecstasy does not stand in disharmony with that of calm.

Then I concluded:

You know, many people think of the church as something more or less fixed and understood: "The church? We know what it is." This goes for people both inside and outside of the church—for those committed to it as for those dismissive of it.

But, really, the church from its beginning at Pentecost until now is a living and growing organism, being built through the fitting together of living stones, as St. Paul says, of people joining together into new unity. As we move beyond the formal adherence to the church into this ever deeper unity of community, the church itself grows and discloses itself in the world in new depth. This mystery of the church and its disclosure in the Holy Spirit is through us—through "two or three" in agreement.

These words return when I look at a typed text. I had forgotten them. But what has remained in memory, indelible in mind and heart, is the preternatural brightness of a Pentecostal day and the gathering of brothers and sisters in agreement in community.

But I have asked myself how this meditation of community could be brought forward so that this experience at the heart of the church might be more and more realized in us, and not just in words (which, like mine in the house at Semkhoz, are only words) but in power and in living knowledge and experience.

This is a question of concern to all Christians—first to those living in community or aspiring to find life in community, and beyond that to all concerned for the Christian future.

In some ways the word *community* has the advantage and disadvantage of being a familiar one with many familiar uses. We are, willy-nilly, thrown back on our familiar understanding in seeking to discover and to live its deep possibility in Christ. Jesus said, "Behold I make all things new," and yet the words of our language become tired and weighed down by associations, in this case stretching from town meetings to Benedictines. Perhaps the making new of language must wait for the making new of space and of time and of all other conditions and yet . . . we wish for a new start in which we can begin the meditation of what it meant two thousand years ago to be gathered of one accord at Pentecost, and of what it means today.

In fact, it seems to me that there is a word that allows us exactly the desired openness, but also has a tradition of rather deep meditation that has not yet defined it or exhausted its possibilities. It is a word for this consequence of Pentecost that we seek to enter and to live with and in. The word is *sobornost.*

This word appeared newly minted in Russia early in the nineteenth century. It is a word said to be hardly translatable. Yet, from its appearance it has drawn the hopes and the aspirations of many, and not only in Russia, to its open promise and undisclosed depth. Hopes for community, for society, for the church, and for the world itself are invoked in the saying of *sobornost.* It is community, and putting language to this word *sobornost,* that this book explores.

Now it is autumn in Semkhoz. The birch trees are tinged with yellow. There is a modest retreat house here now, and the great story that began at Pentecost continues here, where I am writing, and continues wherever you are reading this, oceans away from here. It is the story of agreement and of community.

In the pages ahead I have used a version of the Eastern Church's particular writing style (brief sections, loosely linked, that provide differing angles of approach), through which I hope to give voice to the idea of community and paint a picture of what faith and community can look like. More important, I hope that we will be able to enter into this picture and realize, as it were from within and in a new context, how the mystery of Community is the heart of the Church.

a life together

Part One

a life of all
joined in all

St. Paul, writing to the Corinthians, speaks of Christians as "unknown, and yet well known." We might say the same thing now with a slight change in wording: in every place in the world today, *Christianity* is well known, and yet unknown. It is well known in the sense we all feel that we know what Christianity is, what its possibilities are, what it has to offer, and what it requires. And we either accept that or we don't.

Fr. Alexander Men, priest and architect of the renewal of faith in Russia, had another perspective. "Christianity is in its infancy," he would repeat.

Once seen in this way, our whole perception changes and we see Pentecost not just as a moment in history when the apostles began to speak of Christ and to draw people together into the church, but beyond that, as a moment like the explosion of light at the beginning of the universe that carried in itself the potential of all the galaxies and worlds. Pentecost contains possibility and promise that can only begin to be disclosed. *Christianity is a world to explore, not an heirloom to preserve,* it is something we enter into and discover therein expansion and newness.

Another Russian thinker said that entering the church is "rushing into a new and unknown world." In this phrase we hear the voice of Bede Griffiths from India admonishing his friends on his last day to "serve the Christ who is growing!" The church we thought of as only too well known appears to us as unknown, or rather as a horizon of discovery. And there is no conversation about that discovery, without that of *community* and *unity*.

$\underset{\raise1pt\hbox{—}}{2}$

Sometimes, in order to find out what a thing is, we can best start by seeing what it is not. And in this case we ask what *unity* is not. Among the first of the stories of Genesis is that of a tower built in Babylon, the first of human cities after the great flood. During that time, the story goes on, all peoples spoke one language and lived in one area, and the tower was intended to reach up to the sky and to establish the "name" of its builders so that they not be "scattered on the earth."

The Lord said, "If they do this, it will be only the beginning and they will know no limit." And so the Lord transformed their language so that they could not understand one another. Being now divided by speech, they left off building the tower and spread out over the earth.

The immediate lesson of the text is that the builders sought to make an unlimited future without remembering God and the holy. But beyond this, the story of the tower and the division of languages touches on how misunderstanding and hostility among peoples grow with the inability to communicate. The speaker of another language becomes the stranger, the feared *other*. Further, the story tells what is true—that human arrogance is behind all these divisions of group from group, family from family, person from person.

And yet, is there not the subtext that humanity, united and grounded in God, could indeed rise to the heavens? Is there not a truth within the words that if only men could learn to build as an offering of love and worship and peace, not out of pride and of "showing how great we are," a unified humanity would indeed reach up to and join with God?

The old Tarocco cards of Italy, first of the playing cards, included picture cards likely drawn from the pageants staged in the late Middle Ages, in which costumed figures represented all the aspects of the world. On one of these cards is an image of a great tower struck by lightning. A man and a woman, like Adam and Eve, fall from the breaking tower, which represents all the towers of all the Babylons of human pride.

Yet I have also seen a painting titled *Pentecost* that shows in the foreground a man with hands raised in prayer and in the background a tower struck by lightning. It is the coming of the Holy Spirit who brings an ending, but it is also the Holy Spirit who is the beginning. "Only the hand that erases can write the true thing," said theologian and philosopher Meister Eckhart.

The breaking apart and all the diverse journeys on the face of the earth, from the Garden of Eden and from the place of the abandoned tower, led into all the multiplicity of life that is human history.

What if humanity came together in the light and spirit poured out at Pentecost? Would it not be possible to become of one heart and mind and to discover a unity in the language of the heart taught by the Spirit, to make that society without fragmentation of which the ancients of Babylon dreamed? In such a society all people would find their place, neither lost in the collective, nor alienated and alone outside of it. This ideal acquires an urgency in the age of globalization. Can we live together and together touch the Divine?

In his essay "The Difficult Path to Dialogue: On Graham Greene's Monsignor Quixote," Fr. Alexander Men expresses the urgency with these words:

> Can we, being so different, live on the same planet?

> The Universe, Nature, and according to Christians, Providence, have answered these questions by confronting humanity with the terrible truth. If we cannot, we shall surely perish.

This issue of contemporary urgency found an answer in the ideal of a human spiritual unity called *sobornost.*

Some words are adopted directly from one language into another because they have no easy and natural native equivalent. In the English language we have countless such words and most of these are easy enough to define and grasp even though they fill a space where an English word was lacking. From Russian the words *troika* and *vodka* would be examples of words easily understood although adopted. The word *sobornost* however, adopted in the absence of a native word, is not at all easy to define and grasp, beyond that we know that it refers somehow to unity.

Unity is a very important subject, whether among nations or churches, communities or families, or even within an individual personality. All of these unities in the world seem fragile or in the process of coming about. At moments these unities may appear even as a sort of pipe dream. So if the word *sobornost* brings something that can deepen our understanding of unity, then it is surely worth the effort of delving into this word.

While associations of this word lead in many directions, we will keep circling back to the word itself and to its direct associations and implications. And let this be the hope with which we all—Eastern and Western—enter this study: the meditation of *sobornost* can be a spiritual work that deepens our understanding of, deepens our level of awareness of, as the last book of the Bible says—"what the Spirit is saying to the churches."

3

Sobornost is a word that is old and yet new, even by definition—it develops new meaning still, not only in Russia but in its use and meditation in every land. It contains an idea not yet fully definable and yet which is ancient in its first fullness long before there was a Russia.

Put that way, it sounds like a classical riddle game of the kind that appear in old fairy stories, with the greatest consequences resting on their solution. Except that we have already given away the word that answers the riddle. But often it is from within the answer that further riddles disclose themselves, riddles that we are all now called to work out.

And we are called with an urgency that comes—again in a riddle language—from within ourselves but also from beyond ourselves.

"Sobornost . . . a strange word in this strange land but yet one that is the warp and woof of men's eternal dreams," wrote Catherine de Hueck Doherty, founder of the Madonna House.

4

Sobornost comes from a form of the word *sobornaya*, which is used in the old Russian Slavonic rendering of the Nicean Creed. The Creed of Nicea tells us concerning the church that it is "One," that it is "Holy"—words that we understand up to a point. But the creed continues, saying that the church is "Catholic" (in Greek, *Katholiki*). If a Christian says that his faith is Orthodox and Catholic (something that, historic associations set aside, a Protestant may also choose to say), he is saying that it is the faith that is held by all people everywhere, at all times, in the expression of St. Vincent of Lerins. It is true in its content (Orthodox) and it is universal in its range in space and time and persons (Catholic). And this is the way we understand the word *Catholic*—as "universal."

That same creed, when translated into the language of Christians in Russia, uses the word *sobornaya* for the Greek *Katholiki*. But *sobornaya* does not mean quite the same thing. While it does mean "united," and in that way represents the Greek idea, it is a unity of things in a conciliar form: in a council or coming together or, we might say, in community.

From the adjective *sobornaya*, the noun *sobornost* is made. The adjectival form is the starting point, and a good place to meet this word is in the creed, where it transposes the simple idea of Catholic or universal (perhaps at some expense in universality of vision) into a dynamic mode where we understand universality as an interweaving of relationships.

5

Many Christians everywhere and in all times, in many pews in many sorts of churches, say or sing the creed without dwelling on the details.

However, in the nineteenth century this word *sobornost* became a focus for meditation for a group of Russian thinkers called Slavophils. They are called Slavophil for their emphasis on a spiritual force in the Russian people they saw as greater than that in the people and materialistic culture of the West. They did not look either to the reforms or to the progress coming from the West, or even to the institutions of the Russian State, but they looked to the model of old Russian farming communes as representing the right ideal of society for Russia.

In a sense the Slavophils were anarchists. They cared little for government, or rather, as Constantine Aksakov wrote in the mid-nineteenth century to Tsar Alexander II, they left government to him:

The Russian people do not wish to govern, they desire to preserve for themselves not political but internal communal life. . . . Having thus left the kingdom of this world to the state they, as a Christian people, choose another path: the path to inner freedom and the spirit, the path to the kingdom of Christ. "The kingdom of God is within you."

For Aksakov and the Slavophils, *society* was different from *the state.* The legal system and all the institutional forms of state, and for that matter, of church, was something they saw as alien to the natural life of the human soul gathered in a harmonious communal life.

Aksakov wrote, "The west developed legality because it sensed the lack of justice within itself." In contrast, the Slavophils posited, was *sobornost*: "a spiritual community of many people sharing life," as a Russian dictionary defines it.

Here's a brisk walk-through of some of the formal materials that help us develop the idea of *sobornost*: The Slavophil idea was that in the emerging society of their time (a society that might be said to be fully flowered in our own day), people were increasingly alienated from each other by the rise of individualism that came with the industrial revolution. These thinkers saw in *sobornost* a middle way for humans between the loss of the personal either in collectivism or in alienated individualism. They found in it a model of an ideal communal life.

In looking toward the model, they idealized a life outside of history, taking refuge from it. They saw it as "an unexpected oasis of another world," as Aksakov put it. Yet the desire for another world need not discredit their understanding of the inhumanity of both individualism and collectivism, although the nationalism that came to be associated with the Slavophils reflects a loss of universal catholic imagination—*Katholikos*—what Slavophils would call *sobornaya*.

Through the Slavophils, *sobornost* emerged from being a mere word used in translation of an old creed (and so read or sung by rote) to a flowing and visionary idea reaching out to represent an ideal of Russian life and also to embrace the whole world with a promise of unity.

Later in history we find the word with Nicholas Lossky, where *sobornost* becomes the reconciliation of competing ideas. And at the turn of the twentieth century, the word was used by the great Russian philosopher and man of letters Vladimir Soloviev to represent the ecumenical reunion of Christians. Martin Luther King Jr. and Pope John Paul II were both strongly influenced by understanding ideas of *sobornost*, with John Paul II returning to it in his early years, when he wrote *Person and Act*.

6

"The sum total of all Christians of all ages past and present comprises one indivisible eternal living assembly of the faithful held together just as much by the unity of consciousness as through the unity of prayer," wrote Alexei Khomiakov.

The church is not merely a compartment of life, not just an organization of various centers of authority large and small, but is an organism made up of all Christian people. The hierarchy and structure of the church is secondary to a life that is absolutely organic, a life of all joined in all— "the spiritual communion of all with the plenitude of the whole church," as Khomiakov put it.

"The Church was superseded by community," declared Pavel Florensky, a prominent thinker of the early twentieth century. Reading these words, we are reminded of the parallels of the romantic vision of the confederate agrarian South in America, or the Ubuntu philosophy of the African commune advanced as a social ideal parallel to *sobornost.*

Any existing or formal commune seen as above the church represents more loss than gain of vision. And yet there is something in us that responds to the coming together of persons in a way that is deeper and greater than any ecclesiastical structure.

This response of the heart, not just of the mind, shows us *sobornost* as a riddle, or even a task, given to us by this word appearing in the creed two centuries ago, and beginning to speak to us in a new way.

1

"Sobornost is the 'I' grounded in 'we,'" wrote the philosopher and priest Fr. Sergius Bulgakov. "In this plural unity of the Church—the Body of Christ—lives the Spirit of God."

This coming together of persons poses for us, before any other riddle, the question of how we can have the *I* if we have given up individualism, and how we can have a *we* if we insist on freedom and reject collectivism. Where, beyond high sounding and abstract words, is there an experience that corresponds to this?

Fr. Bulgakov offers important perspective in referring to "the archetypes of the collective unconscious"—which we share and from which our individualities arise. The unity of individuals, united at a deep level before consciousness, but now as the free choice of unique spiritual beings—this is *sobornost,* that "true sobornost of the church which is concerned with the spiritual life above all." His emphasis on the free union of *sobornost* is a unity of love, absolutely opposite to the obligatory unity of the herd, and of collectivism.

In ourselves we have the experience of touching that which comes not from our personal past but from the shared experience of humanity and of all the generations that have gone before us. So when we read the stories of Genesis we meet Abraham and Isaac and Jacob not only as historical figures but in some way, as figures of our own inner life.

That is one dimension, and another opens out when we pray and find that our prayer is really not separate from that of others but indeed is part of a single great prayer. This single prayer is, as the Bible says, that of the Spirit in us all, and of the Lord offering that prayer to the Father. This touching upon the experience of prayer brings us to the place of love, where *I* and *we* are not in conflict. Indeed, as we deepen within ourselves, we may come closer to all others.

So as we understand those things that form our inner life, and as we pray, and as we feel ourselves in the world, we come to awareness of a common shared life. It is not imposed from outside our personal life, and is not threatening to it, but rather wells up from within.

"Think of the life coursing through a mighty tree," says the philosopher Plotinus. A great tree has the most varied life in stem and leaf and branch and bark and root, endless in variety if closely observed and yet that life that enlivens the tree is *a single life*. So with all the lives of people, this endless variety of the pageant of life could not be if there were not a single unified life of God in which it is all grounded.

The grounding of *I* in *we*, then, is not a demand against our nature, but is a coming home. In every case it is through action—in the act of prayer, of contemplation, or in our active relationships—that we know ourselves and others. *Sobornost*, as Bulgakov asserts, is not a passive preservation of truth; it is an act. "Sobornost is life and there is no place in life for immobility," he writes.

Bulgakov's words about the nonpassive nature of *sobornost*, and Plotinus's reminder about the connected nature of a tree and its branches and leaves, shore up with the words Jesus spoke in the fifteenth chapter of John's Gospel about the vine and the branches united in life. "As the branch cannot bear fruit by itself, unless it abides in the vine, neither can you, unless you abide in me. . . . He who abides in me, and I in him, he it is that bears much fruit" (RSV).

8

The idea of *sobornost* came on the scene in the nineteenth century as something new, but it still seems so new today that we continue to struggle to define it in any one word or phrase. Yet *sobornost* is already at the heart of Jesus' teaching, stated fully in Jesus' words in his prayer to the Father in the Gospel of John chapter 17:

> Neither pray I for these alone, but for them also which shall believe on me through their word; That they all may be one; as thou, Father, art in me, and I in thee, that they also may be one in us: that the world may believe that thou hast sent me.

> And the glory which thou gavest me I have given them; that they may be one, even as we are one: I in them, and thou in me, that they may be made perfect in one; and that the world may know that thou hast sent me, and hast loved them, as thou hast loved me. (KJV)

The prayer completes the initiation of Jesus' apostles and all "those who believe through their word." That is to say, it is an initiation of us.

As initiation it is unique in two respects. First, in every tradition an initiation, whether of knowledge or of power, is passed from one individual to another, and often in secret.

Jesus' prayer is one of return to God the Father, but Jesus' initiation is given to a community—because the mystery into which they are being initiated is that of community (or *sobornost*). Earlier in the Gospel of John, Jesus washes his disciples' feet at the Last Supper. He tells the disciples as he washes that they do not yet understand what he has shown them, but as they learn the ways of community they will begin to understand. (And have we yet made more than a beginning of that understanding? Is it not still in its infancy?) He then completes the initiation by showing that serving one another creates a single organic life when he prays, "I in them and Thou in me."

Second, Jesus' initiation of the apostles is not by *knowledge*, as with other human initiations of a rite or secret or the work of a special craft passed down. Knowledge is a good thing, but the initiation of Jesus goes higher—to an initiation in love, and that love is the heartbeat of Jesus' community.

That Thy Love to me may be in them,
and I in them.

Then knowledge becomes knowledge of Love, wisdom becomes wisdom of Love, power becomes power of Love, and all the pulsing, alternating beat of the world's life becomes a heartbeat.

All of *sobornost* is in this prayer that as Romano Guardini says shows "a plenitude of heart that ebbs and flows like the tides of a deep sea." Free now from the concerns of the Slavophils and the voice of philosophers, *sobornost* is the voice of life itself.

The vision of life disclosed by this deepest and first expression of *sobornost* is perhaps a little like the net of Indra. For in the wonderful net of that old Indian god there is a gem at each intersection and in each gem the reflection of every other. It has been said that the net of Indra was created by all the gems together.

But we see in John 17 that the lines that join the gems of Indra's net are not merely lines of mutual reflection but rather lines of love by which each sustains and creates and completes each in the diagram of the Glory (to use John's word here for "Spirit"), and all are created, sustained, and completed in one.

One Prayer, One Love.

And just as persons are known and become knowable in relationship—a fundamental sense of *sobornost*—so, too, the universe is also relational, living by interchange. "In the physical world each being lives and is maintained only by the destruction of others, while in the spiritual world the construction of each personality constructs all, and each lives by the life of all," wrote the Slavophil thinker Ivan Kireyevsky.

How deep and how radical is this idea of human unity as a living organism!

9

The first outward sign at Pentecost was that the apostles, receiving "power from on high" as was promised, spoke boldly of Jesus and his Resurrection to the crowds assembled from all countries for the Pentecost holy day, and each hearer, of whatever native language, was able to understand.

Here we meet a reversal of the division of nations by speech and culture represented in the story of the tower of Babel. As the Eastern hymn of Pentecost expresses it:

> When the All-Highest descended, confounding the tongues, He divided the nations; but when He distributed the tongues of fire, He called all men to unity; wherefore with one accord we glorify the All-Holy Spirit.

The inner dimension of *sobornost* is, as we found in Jesus' prayer in John 17, that of mutual love. "By this all men will know that you are my disciples, if you have love for one another" (John 13:35, RSV).

This, of course, at all times and in all places, is what Christians have attempted and realized in measure, but can we speak of a specially graced period at the beginning of the history of the early church in which we will find that *sobornost*, that love in action, to which Russians will later aspire?

Nicholas Afanasiev (1893–1966) was one influential teacher of the Russian emigration who did identify such a period. In his study of church history and canon law, he found a time of love and shared service to each other and the world that was prior to the coming of law.

"One transcends the imperfect reality in order to seek perfection," he wrote. "The early Church professed this renunciation of the law. . . . The law has been surpassed by the manifestation of the love of the children of God, free in the Spirit and by the Spirit. Love in the New Testament is always linked to the Holy Spirit, who remains even when all else passes away."

This community of love is, for Afanasiev, expressed in the Eucharist: by sharing of bread and wine the church in each locality is a completeness of the whole, like each

gem of Indra's net in which all the others are reflected.
The presidency in the church is that of love, not of law.

Now, to what extent shared life in loving mutual attention
was the daily reality of the early church is not a simple
question. Perhaps Afansiev idealizes the early church
period—yet we do not have full and detailed knowledge
of much in the early church and can risk to read into it our
hopes and expectations.

However we evaluate the thought of Fr. Afanasiev, we have
in the Bible and in extra biblical sources ample record
that from the day of Pentecost Christians undertook the
great experiment of *living by mutual love.* An experiment
that continues to this day.

We can only speak of Pentecost itself to a certain point
because, as we said, it is a beginning almost in the sense of
the first moments of the universe: with an original flash of
light containing in an unapproachable moment the promise of all the stars and galaxies.

Here is the heart of *sobornost*: sharing life together without
any loss of your true self, we are no longer isolated from

each other and no longer isolated from the whole of God's creation. *Sobornost* is an answer, in some way, to Jesus' answer recorded in the Gospel of Thomas to the disciple's question, "How can we enter the Kingdom as little children as you say?"

Jesus answered, "When you make the inner like the outer and the outer like the inner . . . then you will enter the Kingdom."

Or, as Catherine de Hueck Doherty expresses this mystery of going beyond the division of persons and of inner and outer, speaking of another Pentecost—one that is yet to be: "Then the Christian community will come into existence. Then like the Holy Spirit who formed it, it will be a fire burning . . . and from this fire sparks will kindle the whole Earth!"

10

Andrey Rublev's icon *The Holy Trinity* is an amazing act of visual prophecy showing the unity and the flowing life between persons as the three angels at Abraham and Sarah's table under the oak at Mamre. It is a circle set in motion by the inclination of one to another and turning on the chalice. It is the deep unity and relationship of all things. A unity and relationship that is at the beginning and even before the beginning.

This unity—the unity that Jesus prayed we would achieve—is something beyond our selves as we know them, beyond our personalities as we imagine them and act them from day to day. It is a coming into a new world, into air that is easy to breathe.

It is a coming home to our true home, which is that house of God named by Jesus in John's Gospel, chapter 14—a house that is one but has a unique space for each person. A house we are also to prepare here by imaging it and building its image as best we can in this world. A house of hospitality, of prayer for all people.

How many people today, even though they have a home, feel in some deep sense, homeless? Who has not felt this way?

We are on the journey toward home in God's house and yet in *sobornost* may already discover the wonderful peace and freedom of belonging. Of being just where we should be, where we are eternally and already welcome.

The Shaker hymn speaks of this journey when it says:

> 'Tis a gift to be simple
> 'Tis a gift to be free
> 'Tis a gift to come down
> Where we ought to be
> And when we find ourselves
> In that place just right
> We will be in the valley
> Of Love and delight.

Our times surely show us the need for a way beyond the fragmentation of societies, and individuals, and within the human heart. This path, shown by Jesus, himself the Way, neglected for long by the world and even by many in the church, now shows itself again as a way for humanity to achieve a real unity. "We are moving into an age of love," Fr. Alexander Men said, as he himself moved toward love on a journey where *sobornost* called him.

11

Sobornost was the path opened by Jesus for his disciples, a path of community. We have been speaking of community all along. And the life of community is a living out of *sobornost* in its depth. This way of community appears now with a cascade of new forms: There are new religious communities of men and women sharing life and work in one place every day. The Jerusalem Community, for example, or Taize, appear as direct successors to the older and still vital monastic and religious communities. There are also the new intentional communities: San Egideo, Chemin Neuf, Emmanuel, or the groups of Sword of the Spirit, and others.

And then there are groups meeting for study and prayer and caring for each other, and groups of friends hardly aware of calling themselves community and yet entering the world of *sobornost*. Indeed, our ad hoc circle of acquaintances, when regarded *sub species aeternitatis*—in the light of eternity and in its depth—becomes a form of community.

So as we move from contemplation of *sobornost* in the abstract to considering it within our own life journey, we will come, in some form or another, to life in community.

Life in community has a basis in the Bible and that, as the need for community becomes more apparent in our time, has been revived in the church, including through an understanding of *sobornost*. We have seen that all personal life, going back to that of God before the ages, is in relationship.

Let us underline once again that *sobornost* is a journey. So also community life is a journey toward, and an entering into, a space that is immensely greater than the combination of all personal spaces, and into a life that is far more than that of all our separate lives taken together. This means a setting aside of our limits to join with others in this greater life.

We are not there yet; we are on the way. We each make demands of each other in ordinary life, and also within a community. Within the community every response is in freedom, and yet to live as a person of community, we must accept the others with an openness and humility, and sometimes a forgiveness, that we do not learn in society.

It is essential to remain together, in whatever community we find ourselves on our journey, whether it is formal or informal, to hold together on good days and on bad, in tiredness and in difficulty as well as in joy. The community will grow into this fullness of life to the extent that it is able to learn two difficult lessons: First, that in community individual persons ought not be coerced in the name of leadership or by the "mind of the community." And second, that the individual member of the community, made so completely free, should choose fidelity to the sense and will of the others, giving in freedom the obedience that no one can demand of him or her.

The community that lets go even a little of freedom of persons or of fidelity to unity will fall short of *sobornost*, of real community, and will be stopped on its journey.

A journey is made of many steps. Unity is created by many small acts, each a choice. So also unity is broken by small things. We, both in our communities and as individuals, will inevitably go forward and back on our journey. And yet more and more we are called to enter that stream of God's Spirit flowing forward in small acts, fidelities, choices.

And so we make the small choices: To be present to, and with, our brothers and sisters. To build them up, and not tear down. To share what gifts we have, to forgive, to pray, to rejoice in the Lord. A journey of community is a continually renewed choice and step.

<u>12</u>

Now we discover, as we turn from the vast perspective of the Gospels and the vision Christian thinkers have attached to *sobornost*, that we have become a bit hesitant.

We look from the ideal to the reality of our world and churches and spiritual families and something does not quite fit. We feel, perhaps, like Don Quixote when Sancho Panza tried to pass off a plain village girl as the Dulcinea del Toboso of his dreams. We want to see the real person, but, no, we do not.

We do not see it.

That the idea of *sobornost* developed in Russia among a group of Russian thinkers does not mean that we can find the full working model of this reconciliation and unity if we simply go to an Eastern Orthodox Church.

The French priest and thinker Fr. Lev Gillet aligned himself with Orthodoxy partly in response to this deep and stirring idea the Slavophils held about *sobornost*. But he came to see—as he witnessed disputes among émigré Russians in Paris, where some held *sobornost* merely as a slogan—a lack of true kindness and mutual support of *sobornost* as a living principle.

Was it disillusioning? Perhaps, in a way, but might not freedom from the illusion be a step toward the real thing?

Theologian Dietrich Bonhoeffer, in his book *Life Together*, which comes out of a community of study underground in the time of the Nazi regime, emphasizes the absolute importance of staying with only the real:

> By sheer grace, God will not permit us to live even for a brief period in a dream world. He does not abandon us to those rapturous experiences and lofty moods that come over us like a dream. God is not a God of the emotions but the God of truth. Only that fellowship which faces such disillusionment, with all its unhappy and ugly aspects, begins to be what it should be in God's sight, begins to grasp in faith the promise that is given to it. The sooner this shock of disillusionment comes to an individual and to a community the better for both.

So a young couple, who are so fortunate as to feel a deep first love in which the other seems an ideal prince or princess, quickly enough, and in some ways the sooner the better, come to see that the real beloved is not an ideal but is a real person whose limits and blemishes cannot be ignored or wished away. A real relationship of love cannot be just a fairy tale and yet . . . beyond the first illusion and then the disillusion there stands open a life of love for a real prince and princess. The disillusion is not, and does not need to be, the last word.

It is the same with communities. Yes, we find in existing communities the same sorts of human situation arising that, if we are looking to the ideal of *sobornost*, can lead to a feeling like that of Don Quixote when reproving his well-intentioned friend Sancho for offering him the village milkmaid as his ideal Dulcinea.

But need we then abandon *sobornost* as a dream of ivory-tower intellectuals? Is it a doomed attempt to bring into history something—the kingdom of God—that must remain outside of history?

Perhaps now we may think it would be easier to give up
the whole thing as a bad job and stick to what is tan-
gible and easily demonstrable. But then what of *sobornost's*
startling fidelity to the words of Jesus on the Mount of
Olives? We dare not dismiss them as a mere dream. We
know them to be a prophetic opening out of the inner
truth of human life, and yet . . .

Here we come to a depth of the riddle presented to us by
sobornost.

On the one hand we dare not offer clouds for food to
people, including ourselves, needing bread. On the other
we can hardly, without despair, let go of the ideal.

Let us say, provisionally, that the idea of *sobornost* is not an
unrealizable ideal, because we sense it at moments of clear
breathing under blue inner sky, and we feel it realized in
moments of shared life. Yet it comes to us as a call from
the future, from the end, the omega point if you will, of
the journey. And this understanding imposes a condition
on what we can expect in ourselves, our churches, our
communities.

 B

Simeon L. Frank, perhaps the greatest of the Russian thinkers, said that *sobornost* is about the joining of the *I* and the *we* (we are reminded of the words of the twentieth-century philosopher of the Russian emigration Nikolai Berdyaev: "*sobornost* is the 'I' grounded in the 'we'"). Neither one has priority, they are a dual unity, *I* and *we*, but this unity is only possible in God, the source of both, which can only be realized in service.

Before full sunrise the light of dawn touches the tops of hills with brightening glints of a coming day. So it is with *sobornost*—a promise for the future but blessedly not without example. Even now we witness lives in service and shared mutual giving of and to each other and to God.

Mother Maria Skobtsova is an example of this concept in a life of service. She ran a soup kitchen for the poor and a house of hospitality for refugees. You could say that hospitality was the heart of her approach to others. When the Nazis came to Paris, that service of hospitality meant serving and saving as best she and her coworkers could, the Jewish people. She died giving her life for another in the concentration camp at Ravensbrück—an expression of her understanding of *sobornost.*

"[*Sobornost*] is not an abstraction or a higher reality with no inner connection to the individual human beings who constitute it," she wrote. "It is a reality because each is that soul which is worth the whole world. . . . In communing with the image of God, we commune with God . . . an authentic mysticism of communing with man [that is] another form of communing with God."

Far from the Slavophil definition of *sobornost* in terms of Russian land and folk culture, the whole of humanity is now *sobornost's* scope. Mother Skobtsova said, "If we were true Christians, we would all wear the star of David."

British writer Charles Williams provides another example of the application of *sobornost* in his own writings. Williams does not use the word *sobornost* at all, and his contact with Russian thought was in no way formative, but his own theology revolved around the concept of "co-inherence"— in essence a parallel and even identical thought to *sobornost.* He wrote of "the practice of substituted love" according to (in another Williams expression) "the pattern of the Glory." He proposed and initiated an "Order of the Co-inherence" whose purpose was to "meditate and practice" the way of shared life, of exchange and substituted love.

Williams's essay "The Way of Exchange" concludes with these words:

> The good works which thou hast prepared for us to walk in are those that belong to "that holy fellowship"; they are therefore peculiarly those of exchange and substitution. They are there and they are prepared, we have only to walk in them. A little carrying of the burden, a little allowing our burden to be carried; a work as slow, as quiet, even as dull as the agreement to take up or give up a worry or a pain, a compact of substitution between friends—this is the beginning of the practice. The doctrine will grow in us of itself.

A person in panic about an upcoming interview is an example of Williams's co-inherence, as a friend sets that anxious person free by taking on that panic himself. It is clear that Williams is directly working with the heart of *sobornost*—in the command to bear one another's burdens and in the words, "he saved others, himself he cannot save," used by Williams as a charter of interdependence— in a way that no other writer, including the Russians, has done.

Perhaps the awkwardness, if it is that, of the examples of exchanged love arises because it is a doctrine that, like *sobornost* itself, is only beginning to grow in the church. Williams says that if we act in terms of co-inherence, of *sobornost*, "the doctrine will grow in us of itself."

14

We are one in the Spirit, we are one in the Lord.

We are one in the Spirit, we are one in the Lord.

And we pray that all unity may one day be restored.

And they'll know we are Christians

By our love, by our love,

Yes they'll know we are Christians by our love."

Peter Scholte's song expresses the natural idea that not only are Christians committed to love one another, but also that this love should have the consequence of bringing together Christian churches into ecumenical unity.

We may ask what *sobornost* offers to this search for unity. The Slavophils first enunciated *sobornost* outside the church, looking to a fullness of truth in their own spiritual and social tradition.

But Vladimir Soloviev adopted the idea of *sobornost* within a different and overarching vision. He wrote to a friend, "I am as far removed from Latin limitations as I am from Byzantine limitations or the Augsburg or Geneva ones.

The religion of the Holy Spirit which I profess is wider and of a fuller content than all separate religions: it is neither the sum total nor the extract of the separate organs."

Soloviev devoted great attention to the problem of finding a *sobornost,* a unity in diversity, of the historical churches. His *Russia and the Universal Church* expresses a vision of global, political, social, spiritual, and even political unity. He came to feel, however, that his immediate suggestions of Christian unity could not be achieved. The pope of that time, responding to Soloviev's work, called this vision "a beautiful idea but impossible to realize short of a miracle." In a late work, "Short Story of the Antichrist," Soloviev sees Christian unity as arising not so much from any great plan but from the joining together of Christian persons.

In this story, the unity of the church is realized through three figures: Professor Pauli, the Elder John, and Pope Peter II. For Soloviev, these three represent the great streams of Christianity—Protestant, Orthodox, and Catholic—harkening back to the theologian Paul, the beloved disciple John, and the rock Peter.

If in our day it seems that formal ecumenism reaches its limits just as surely as Soloviev's large and detailed plans for world unity, it remains that there is another way to unity. The way of Peter, Paul, and John: three persons coming together within the love of God. Where the ecumenism of discussion and dialectic comes to an end, there is another ecumenism possible, which we will now go on to consider: the ecumenism of *sobornost* as friendship.

15

If we go back to the root of the idea of *sobornost* in the Gospels and then ask ourselves how *sobornost* would most basically express itself in the coming together of Christian churches in ecumenism, the answer is clear.

It would be in love. In an ecumenism of love and friendship.

Fr. Pavel Florensky, that many-sided genius spoken of earlier, sometimes called the Russian Leonardo da Vinci, included an essay on friendship in his *Pillar and Ground of the Truth*, a unique book made up of twelve letters. His letter on friendship is an important expression of the idea of *sobornost* in the sense of Christian love infused with divine grace. Florensky gives us an extended and deep consideration of love in the form of friendship that fits within the unfolding of the Gospel that is *sobornost*.

His letter does not have a formal structure but is a series of insights set out and developed before moving on to the next flash of thought. In this way it corresponds to the structure of John 17 itself, and perhaps represents the only way in which the mind can deeply approach ideas that are almost beyond expression and so present themselves as intuitions:

> Life is a continuous series of dissonances.
> But through friendship they are resolved.
>
> Similarity and nonsimilarity, or oppositeness,
> are equally necessary in friendship.
>
> It is necessary to illuminate and suffuse each day
> with closeness.

Perhaps Fr. Florensky's most important emphasis, from the point of view of our exploration of *sobornost*, is that the basic unit of the church is not the isolated individual but the individual within friendship, and the church itself a network of friendships:

> The friendly structure of the . . . community of Christians characterizes not only [their] relation to the center, but also the smallest fragments. Like a crystal, a Christian community is not fragmented

into amorphous, noncrystalized parts. . . . The limit to fragmentation is not the human atom, but a community molecule, a pair of friends.

The French theologian Olivier Clement continues to express the thought of Florensky: "If we recall that Jesus sent his disciples in pairs, we realize that friendship goes beyond all (merely formal and therefore heavy) group dynamics, which can be the limit," he says, "of some theologians' vision of the Church's reality."

Florensky saw how the church is built on "the crossing of numerous friendships," an idea that is the basis of the ecumenical thought and work of French Orthodox theologian Antoine Arjakowsky, director of the Institute of Ecumenical Studies at the Catholic University in Lviv, Ukraine—a country positioned between the Eastern and Western churches and also between the cultures of Eastern and Western Europe. "Here in Lviv we are in a historical zone of extraordinary encounter between East and West, and at the same time of painful fracture between Christians. That is why we attach great importance to the establishing of the close association of Christian university members who belong to different denominations."

Arjakowsky calls "ecumenism based on friendship" the "ecumenism of Life," which is neither denominational nor ethnic. "We have to communicate broadly and yet speak intimately."

The institute in Lviv is an extraordinary sign of hope in the Christian world, and represents a direct application of the love of *sobornost* of brothers and sisters within a network of *philia*, of friendship. This could be one way to live out the conclusion of Peter Scholte's song: "We will walk with each other, / We will walk hand in hand. / And together we'll spread the News / that God is in our land."

16

Again we turn to the beginning of the human story when myth and reality were one, when the tower of Babel was abandoned and humanity was scattered over the face of the earth, when history began.

As we experience them, breakdown and division are certainly destructive and even tragic. But they are also part of the creation of the world and of persons. This is a point of enormous importance and one that is deeply encouraging as we consider our own lives and the divisions in the world and among Christians.

Fr. Alexander Men, in his "Two Understandings of Christianity," expresses concisely and with a clarity I have not seen anywhere else how this is reflected in the history of the church:

> And it seems to me that such pluralism, such interaction of different points of view, is an important pre-condition for the vitality of Christianity. And perhaps it was providential that Christianity was

split into different tendencies, because without this it would probably have been something uniform and forced. It is as if, knowing people's tendency to intolerance, God divided them so that each person in their place, in their own garden could bring forth their own fruit.

The journey of synthesis is our history—of humanity, of the church—and in the thought of *sobornost* we have traced one path: "And the time will come," Fr. Men continues, "when all the different fruits will come together into one stream, in which will be preserved all the best in the spiritual culture of humanity and of each person who is made in the image and likeness of God."

All suffering, then, is not just something to endure but is part of the making of things, it is "creative suffering" (the title of the admirable little book by Julia de Beausobre, a spiritual writer of the Russian emigration). In the end, indeed it can be as Goethe says, that "all our strife, all earthly care" is part of "God's eternal peace."

Long ago, Origen, of third-century Alexandria, expressed it this way: "There spring from one beginning many differences and varieties, which again, through the goodness of God, and by subjection to Christ, and through the unity of the Holy Spirit, are recalled to one end."

Even earlier, in the first century of Christianity, Hermas, an otherwise unknown Christian living in Rome, returning to the place where myth blends seamlessly into reality, saw this synthesis in a vision.

Indeed, in its beginning this vision subtly reminds us of a question: Is *sobornost* something we can really see? Or is it largely an unrealized abstract idea? So with Hermas's vision. The lady who was his mystagogue and guide moved a wand in the air and asked him what he saw.

"I see nothing."

"Do you not see a tower?"

He saw.

He saw a great and radiant tower being built on the face of the waters being constructed one stone at a time. The stones that fit together were being first put in place and the ones that would not fit being separated out and worked with so that large or small they would all fit in some place in the tower. Where then:

all agreed with one another and had peace with one another. . . . That is why their joints fit together in the building of the tower.

17

I said in the beginning that *sobornost* is a riddle, a word hardly translatable from its original Russian and yet not fully mined or understood in Russian either.

An ordinary riddle can be answered in a way that dissolves the riddle. A secret can be told. An allegorical parable can be explained and reduced to its correspondences.

But although *sobornost* is a word, the riddle we are advancing is not really one of words but of persons and their relations. That, of course, is quite a different sort of thing, and one that necessarily passes into mystery. And this mystery presents itself to the person not as an external problem, but as from within the living of one's days.

If sobornost is this sort of riddle, that of persons in the mystery of their inward being, then the solution must also be inward. The words Rainer Maria Rilke wrote to a young poet may then resonate:

Have patience with everything that remains unsolved in your heart. Try to love the questions themselves, like locked rooms and like books written in a foreign language. Do not now look for the answers. They cannot now be given to you because you could not live them. It is a question of experiencing everything. At present you need to live the question. Perhaps you will gradually, without even noticing it, find yourself experiencing the answer.

Indeed, R. M. Rilke's words, as written in his "Letter to a Young Poet," coincide to our finding that *sobornost* is a journey and is known in experience.

It is time now to draw together all our threads of definition of *sobornost* and see just what we are left with.

18

Sobornost is ongoing in its definition. We cannot give final definition to it because it continues in relationship and in movement and in exchange.

Therefore, when it is said that *sobornost* is untranslatable, surely this is partly because its meaning is unfixed and is developing. A translation is imprecise because the word is in motion, like those electrons that quantum science does not allow us to call either particles or a wave.

In part the riddle of *sobornost* lies in its being, as we have said, something hardly exemplified except at graced moments. The defining of *sobornost*, then, depends on awareness of and openness to these moments—and prior to that, on the choice to be open to these moments by an inner disposition of availability. So also Plato, having set forth his vision of the Republic, which itself is a society built on *sobornost*, one might say, raises the objection that such a society can be found nowhere on earth. But, he replies, we may contemplate the Republic, and by contemplation, and in our lives, constitute ourselves citizens of it.

In this aspect of individual choice and action, *sobornost* is theologian Reinhold Niebuhr's "impossible possibility" of applying love to social interrelations. It is also what my friend Andrey Cherniak, of the contemporary Russian group Hosanna, likes to express in relation to life in community: often it is impossible but still absolutely necessary.

The riddle remains, to the end, a riddle, a paradox, worked by choice, but also worked together. This second aspect of the resolution of the riddle is collective. It is what Catherine de Hueck Doherty refers to when she calls the task of *sobornost* that of "forging a chain of hearts," saying that they "will blend with the heart of Christ. That is restoration. That is healing. That is sobornost."

Which brings us to *sobornost* as a task of the church. *Sobornost* and community, while not a "church within the church," may open a perspective of the church beyond the existing church and toward which we already journey.

Now here is part of the ongoing riddle of *sobornost*: if the existing church were to suddenly become fully aware of the church that is coming, of the spiritual communion of all with all, what things would change and what would remain the same in the church today?

We might look to history as a window to that riddle. History proposes certain problems to the church. For example, the early Methodists faced the problem of mission on the American frontier and had to adapt the structure of their church to it. So also the church will need to make changes if, or perhaps when, humanity moves out into space on the road to the stars. As Trappist monk Thomas Merton said, using an image of yaks carrying monastery treasure across a river in Tibet, "I don't think in the next 50 years we will be able to get all our yaks across the river."

But the question of *sobornost* arises, as it were, not from outside, but from the depth of the church's self-consciousness. In a real way the question that rises from within the church's consciousness can create difficulties because it is, as we said, of the mystery of personal being, not approachable simply by words or definition. It is learned, as Rilke said, only in experience, only on the journey.

The Question that comes from within.

As *sobornost* gently knocks on each closed door and offers an invitation into a larger space, does it not also offer a challenge to each of our lives and to the lives of our formal or informal communities? This challenge rises from the future, but also from the depth of the heart, and it is a profound challenge to our way of structuring life.

In any case, the definition of *sobornost* and the question it raises, grows and deepens from step to step as we follow on, but we know that the end of community and of *sobornost* is personal, is revealed in a person—the person of the Lord, who spoke of how all people might be one:

> He is going before you . . .
> There you will see him,
> as he told you.

Though we have reached the conclusion of this section, it is appropriate for us to go further in discovering and applying *sobornost* in our lives. We will approach this task on three levels, which I refer to as the Ways of *Sobornost*— the Ways of the Practice of Friendship, you might say:

first, in learning *seeing;* second, in realizing *complementarity;* and third, in realizing *mission* at its depth, where mission is grounded in prayer.

Part Two

seeing

You could say that the whole of life essentially lies in *seeing*. Philosopher Teilhard de Chardin wrote, "To be more is to be more united. But unity grows, and we will affirm this again, only if it is supported by an increase of consciousness, of vision." These words of Teilhard touch a theme central to Christianity, to unity, to *sobornost*: that of watchfulness. However, there is no simple history to the Christian response to Jesus' command in Mark's Gospel to "watch." This, too, is part of the contemporary situation in which we explore the way to *sobornost*, and it deserves our consideration.

The historical development of the church shows what has been called "the ages of the spiritual life," with their gain and loss similar to what we observe in the life of an individual.

Now in our age, where information is so fully available, we have the opportunity to reflect on what can be the complete wholeness of the spirituality of the church incorporating all of that history.

The theme introduced by Teilhard's words is a prime example of this. Jesus, as is recorded in Mark 13:37, tells the apostles, "What I say to you I say to all: Watch!" (RSV). It is a command to alertness to the events of the world that is also directly oriented toward the Eschaton, the End, the "Day of the Lord," which will bring all things to their ends. Of this we do not know the day and hour, and so must be alert. It could be said that this attitude of watching picks up the word to the prophet Ezekiel, "Son of man, I have made you as a watchman" (Ezekiel 3:17; 33:7, RSV). For the early Christians, the dimension of watching for the coming of the Lord also included the watching of the world, because there is a darkness that seeks to destroy and so in our time in history we must "be sober, be vigilant" (1 Peter 5:8, KJV).

However, this alertness of the early church became obscured, and not simply because of a loss of the sense that the Lord was returning immediately. Historically, this vision was obscured because in the Christian tradition, and in the Eastern Orthodox tradition specifically, there was a reordering of the command to vigilance and watchfulness into a watching of interior states, which was first exemplified in monastics. Thus *nepsis,* the Greek for "watchfulness" or "vigilance," become primarily an ascetic terminology for an inward attention.

So St. Symeon the New Theologian says: "Our whole soul should have at every moment a clear eye, able to watch and notice the thoughts entering our heart from the evil one and repel them. The heart must be always burning with faith, humility and love. Do not fear the conflict, and do not flee from it; where there is no struggle, there is no virtue."

This inner work is the praxis of Evagrius in the desert, and "the solitary battle inwardly against demons" of St. Nil

Sorski. St. Nil simplified the outer forms of the monastic life in order to allow full range for the individual development of each monk through *nepsis*. The result is that watchfulness becomes, first of all, a matter of the interior life. This produces an awareness of psychology and of the interior life that is profound, but at the cost of the setting aside of the original eschatological orientation of vision. The original expectation toward the coming Christ was replaced, on the one hand, by the Christian empire, and on the other hand, by the maximal inner effort of the Desert Fathers. Watching was, in the desert, turned inward. And while the Christian empire engaged in the world, it also resigned itself to going with the way of the world to a considerable extent.

The development of liturgy in a mysterial direction removed it from the people, a development with different specifics in East and West but with the similar result of infrequent communions and the rise of clericalism. The liturgical renewal beginning in the nineteenth century brought back frequent communion in much of the Christian world, but where do we see a recovery of the original orientation of the interior life?

In our time, however, there seems to be signs of the recovery of the original sense of watchfulness among masters of the interior life. Let us represent this by three quotations that reflect the three dimensions of seeing. These fulfill the Gospel command to "watch," and do so in terms that are deeply contemporary.

First, in his journals, Fr. Alexander Schmemann, the great Orthodox spokesman of liturgical renewal, says that his sense of deepest peace comes at moments when he focuses on the things around him, as he "sees the truth of sky and wet branches and foggy dusk." To that he adds, "The mystic is the one who does not close his eyes but who sees." This seeing of the world that God has made for us to live in is surely one dimension of watching.

A second dimension of watching is that which Teilhard de Chardin opens out when he says that it is characteristic of our time that there is an explosion of knowledge and indeed wonderful and wonder-inducing new awareness of the world as science opens to us, through telescope and microscope. But what he says is spiritually decisively important in that we see in this the glory of Christ through whom the worlds were made. If we see in this way, our new knowledge of the world will be focused anew on Christ.

Then a third dimension of watching comes from the spiritual master and theologian Fr. Sergius Bulgakov, whom we have already met along our way. Fr. Bulgakov said, "So apocalyptic is my attitude towards life that (even when lonely in my position in the Church or in a sense left unsatisfied by its history) I am supremely joyful. . . . I grasp the meaning of events finding in them the fulfillment of the promised future." He added that "it is this focus on the Lord who is coming that makes me feel entirely at home with everything and everyone around me in the Church." Here we see the watching and seeing focused on Christ, who frees us to see our own time and place at work for the building of the church.

To these three dimensions of seeing we might add as method the words of Simone Weil, another spiritual master of our time: that what our time needs is a recovered discipline of *attention*, which makes it possible to see. And it is "absolutely unmixed attention," she wrote, that "is prayer."

Here we have an outline of seeing and watching—or *nepsis*—which brings us back toward the Gospels' centeredness on the coming Christ in terms that rise from the experience of life and the world God gives us today.

We said that the idea of watching, of *nepsis*, as an internal discipline of vigilance was part of the development of monastic communities in the church. Can we expect that the opening out of this emphasis on seeing, returning to the seeing of the world and of our times and of the Lord as coming through all, may bring with it a new development in monasticism? A new understanding of community?

Indeed there is a moving in our time in the appearance of new communities and in the spread of the idea of Christian community beyond the formal monastic community. St. Tikhon of Zadonsk spoke of "interior monasticism," saying, prophetically, at the end of the eighteenth century that in the time that was coming, this joining of monastic spirit to life in the world would be of the utmost importance. And indeed now we see new Christian communities, movements, and brotherhoods in both East and West that are beginning to show the way toward interior monasticism, in a corporate practice of watching and seeing.

In addition to liturgical renewal, in the last century we have seen—both West and East—a recognized need for a parallel renewal deepening the inner and corporate life: a looking toward that completion of both that *sobornost* promises.

If we follow these directions into the future, then surely individuals and communities within the church will find a wholeness of vision, joining that of the past to that of our time and into the future, a wholeness promised from the beginning in the command of Jesus: "What I say to you, I say to all—watch!"

As we watch for the coming Lord, our prayer becomes joined to that most ancient of Christian prayers, Maranatha ("Even so, come, Lord Jesus"). Our intercession claims that toward which we are looking: the promise of the Lord for the future. In the words of theologian Walter Wink, intercessory prayer is a spiritual claim "in the name of what God has promised" and of the future that he gives.

Part Three

each complete
in the other

thirty sections on complementarity

The opening out of the concept of *complementarity* in our time offers another path toward the unity of *sobornost*. Complementarity is the completion of opposites in each other, each necessary to the other and relying on the other. It is the deep interrelation and mutual dependence of all things. In physics it is the need for both *wave* and *particle* to describe atomic phenomena that is a central intuition of quantum physics. Perhaps the word *complementarity* is too large, but no other word incorporates the larger meaning. St Paul's words come to mind as analogous: "Let each now not look to his own things but to those of the other."

Complementarity, by definition, is not a linear subject matter. For that reason I am using the approach of paragraphs circling and triangulating our subject in the manner of the early church fathers, writing as they did in loosely linked paragraphs—each, as it were, complete in the other.

1

Niels Bohr found that when a scientist set up an experiment to measure light as a wave, it would manifest as a wave, and when using a measuring instrument to measure for particles, light would manifest as particles. These are alternate and mutually exclusive descriptions of the phenomena and each is complete in itself. And the experimenter's choice of experiment enters into the result.

If we set up the experiment so as to know where an object is, we screen out the information related to its energy and movement, and vice versa. Yet the light measured is both particle and wave, and has both location and energy, though these cannot be contained in a single experiment.

2

Bohr thought that this discovery was not simply a
question of descriptions of light but of all phenomena.
He suggested that complementarity exists not only in the
world of physics but in every area of life and experience.
Bohr makes it a general philosophical principle. Indeed,
he adopted for his personal coat of arms the Chinese
yin-yang symbol of complementarity of opposites, with
the subscript *contraria sunt complementa* (opposites are
complementary).

3

Andrey Cherniak of the Hosanna Community in Russia has a background in chemistry, working in the Russian space program before becoming a full-time Christian worker. He likes to invoke complementarity as opening the way for theology in every area. Although, as he says, virtually no theology has tried to enter this new land.

For him, the complementarity of all Christian groupings, or denominations, calls us to consider in sets of two, or indeed as a whole, each with all.

Like an experiment that gives some data but screens others, all seem to be complete systems (well, some very logically complete, such as Neo-Thomism or Calvinism) and within each there seems no other possible solution! We meet this in any discussion between those in one world of thought with those in another. And yet in order to come into contact with reality beyond system, we need them all.

4

Suppose complementarity to be ground where there are divisions between the churches—where does that leave our familiar theologies and traditions? A friend deeply committed to the ecumenical movement remarked of a mutual acquaintance with surprise, "You know, that man really believes that we and (the members of another church) are one church. But if that were true, then we would then have nothing to talk to each other about!"

5

Fr. Alexander Men spoke of a young man who felt that his only choice was between being an Orthodox who condemned Baptists, or a Baptist who could not recognize the Orthodox. (We all have met this young man and his brothers and sisters.) This is a fear of losing boundaries and distinctions, like that of a person afraid to go out of his own house. As Fr. Men said, "There is a psychological disease called agoraphobia, the fear of space. It seems the Tsar Peter suffered from this; he always built himself little houses and little rooms. Well this sickness exists also in the history of religions."

<u>6</u>

To my friend concerned that if we were already one there would be nothing to talk about, I reply "Well, we could pray!"

7

But we could also imagine a use of theological systems, and ways of worship and prayer, not for the purpose of argumentation, nor comparisons nor "show and tell," as at a certain period of ecumenical activity, but as complementary thought and prayer received each by all, and together moving toward that which is beyond the reach of any alone. *Sobornost.*

8

Knowledge of the parts involves knowledge of the whole: "One needs two ears to determine where a sound is coming from," says Andrey Cherniak, "and this is true for hearing what God is speaking to the churches today."

9

To bear one another's burdens and so to fulfill the law—
the call of *sobornost*—also means a complementarity in
healing. For each spiritual family is scarred and wounded,
and in this light of complementarity we see the other in
a new way and do not so easily move into accusation of
error. As it is written of the mote and the beam: only the
Baptist can bear the burden of what the Orthodox has
made of his history, and only the Orthodox that of what
the Baptist has made of his.

10

How can theology, as the working together of complementary systems, of Calvinist and Arminian, of Thomist and Palamite, become a divine play in which all move together toward an end beyond the range of any in separation?

11

I have seen the model in Bible study. After a discussion on the first chapter of Revelation with a group of many backgrounds (Orthodox, Catholic, Baptist) in Moscow, all Bible teachers, I remark how the exchange seemed like a kind of wonderful play. A friend replies, "We are all teachers. We are free to propose ideas which might be wrong or heretical and to consider them and turn them around. No one will be shocked or frightened. It is a very wonderful time of spiritual relaxation for us."

<u>12</u>

This model of play in discussion of Scripture may be more common among Jewish students. The *Zohar* (The Book of Splendor) is a divine play of Bible interpretation, a play that leads the rabbis to shedding many tears of awe at the wonder of what discloses through the sharing of thought.

𝕭

The five sages, it is said in the Passover Haggadah, passed the whole night in talk of the mystery of freedom, so absorbed that they scarcely noted the dawn. Nor was Reb Akiva intent on convincing Reb Shimon, or Reb Shimon on convincing Reb Eleazer, of anything, but the sages worked together in awe and depth.

14

"And there will be a glorious dance of praise!" writes Mechthild of Magdeburg. It will be a dance "from love into knowledge, from knowledge into joy, from joy beyond all human senses."

15

"Say Amen to me!" cries Jesus to the disciples in an ancient hymn, as he leads them in a round dance. "To each and all it is given to dance. Amen. / Who does not dance has missed the reality. Amen."

16

In daring to approach theology in a new way, we are not simply enlisting in the Copenhagen Interpretation (where Bohr and Heisenberg forged the new scientific paradigm beyond that of Einstein), but moving in that sacred ground of riddle play we see in *sobornost*, in the play of children in shoemaker mystic Jacob Boehme's sunny fields. We see it in our own experiences also: a Bible study in Moscow or New York, or in a room at dusk with a young man softly singing the songs of John Wimber, or in a dance around the Sabbath table.

<u>17</u>

The two cherubs of Eden guard the tree planted in the formless and void. Their swords polarize and divide all into positive and negative, back and forth, like lightning descending, ionizing. Is there no way between?

18

Two pillars, Joachim and Boaz, frame the sides of the Temple of Solomon. Two dogs on the sides of a Japanese gate, one mouth open pronouncing the first sound *aaaa*, the other with mouth closed humming the last *nnnn*. Alpha and Omega.

<u>19</u>

The two cherubs of Eden now wait beside a door into empty space that had been a tomb (Luke 24). There is resolution in the center, not as an averaging or even transcending synthesis (*auftgehoben*), but as resurrection. In that empty space, resolution.

<u>20</u>

Poet Boris Pasternak gives to Jesus these words: "They shall cast me into such a void that I shall attain my full stature."

21

"We must turn physics around," David Bohm, a twentieth-century physicist, insists, "instead of starting with parts and showing how they relate, we must start with the whole."

22

Nicholas de Cusa, that astonishing Christian philosopher of the fifteenth century, proposed a unity of opposites, perhaps giving us a foothold in the theology to come. For him, the world is an interplay of opposites. In perceiving this interplay, we discover also our own limitation (learned ignorance) and realize that the final reconciliation of the opposites is only in the infinity of God.

This unity of opposites goes far beyond the reconciliation of churches.

23

We find ourselves between the photon and the star, between your mind and mine, in the ebb and flow that is the pulse of the universe. Do we not now divine that ebb and flow relate to the beat of the heart of the Lord as John felt it, resting his head on the Master's chest at the Last Supper?

24

The call is to go forward with authentic spirit and without illusion or succumbing to mirages.

25

In the book of Revelation we meet images of resolution:
resolution of a sea mingled with fire (15:2) as of the two
triangles of David's Star. And in the great city that is coming, there is found neither day nor night (neither particle
nor wave), but "the Lord gives light."

26

So we return once more to Fr. Alexander Men's words that
it was the separation of Christians that allowed all the
aspects implicit in the explosion of light that was Pentecost
to be seen without one overwhelming the others. Here is
complementarity in action, "The time will come when all
the different fruits will come together into one stream, in
which will be preserved all the best in the spiritual culture
of humanity and of each person who is made in the image
and likeness of God. As it is written: 'For he is our peace,
who hath made both one,'" Fr. Men wrote.

Two cherubs, swords now drawn back. The tomb is full
of light.

<u>27</u>

On the new Jerusalem, the poet Chico Martin writes: "In the image of God's kingdom revealed as a city, where we have previously remarked on the proximity of the boundaries between heaven and earth, we now have a vision without boundary at all. . . . A vivid image of two bodies which do in fact occupy the same space at the same time. Heaven and earth, the kingdom of God and the kingdom of the world: one appearance that can be described two ways."

28

Here, a paraphrase of the words the great angel spoke to John at the end of the book of Revelation (22:11–13): "Look into my face and see the End. To all that was well done, and all that you did poorly. To what you desired to be and to what you became. To the right and the left, the inner and the outer, to the contraries between which you have made your way. For I am coming and I bring in my hand that which all men seek in all their dreams and all their days, and which is the End of all things."

<u>29</u>

On the eve of Pentecost and on retreat, in a wood outside
Moscow, and on a day when the light falls through absolutely clear air, a friend sleeps briefly and dreams: "I saw
a great Chalice and I knew that in it the opposites and all
contradictions are resolved, it is Marriage, and also it is
the mystery of community . . . it is the Grail."

30

So we come by the path of complementarity to a place where again we envision the unity that is *sobornost*. In following that path into the reality of the complementarity of *sobornost*, there remains for us first the work of prayer.

> *Lord, you alone our light, our light beyond knowledge, and before and after our poor and varied perception, shine on our path, let us not stray in devious ways. Let us find the path to the place of meeting, where you bring things to their ends and show them reconciled. Reconciling our broken and wounded hearts, touch also our minds and make us vessels of that same and true integration that is both healing and light beyond differentiation.*
>
> *Amen.*

Part Four

prayer and mission

We pass from consideration of complementarity now into prayer, and in our meditation of *sobornost* it is time to follow prayer into mission, for mission is a conversation, and also a deeply working expression of, and achievement of, *sobornost*.

It is conventional but also true to say that our lives today are fragmented. Perhaps it is true of the lives of all people in all times, but perhaps the fragmentation is a little accentuated in our time by the speed and availability of information, by the numbers of people that we meet in person, by cell phone, by Internet. And all of these meetings make demands on our life, pulling us in various directions. Our day is divided between these many needs, and at the end of meeting each need it can seem that there is nothing that remains just for ourselves.

When we experience things in this way, then in the midst of all activities and meetings we will feel a futility, an emptiness.

Now as Christians we understand that mission is something that we should do—that we should represent Christ to other people and tell them of the risen Lord. And at the same time if we are to tell a person something, we must have a relationship, which means we must also listen.

The church must listen to the world. To really listen is to accept that we may hear something of value, it cannot be just listening in order to get to the next stage of the argument we are presenting. In biblical terms, this is to accept that we are completed in the other: "Bear one another's burdens," "Let each look not on his own but on those of the other."

If mission is a listening as well as a speaking, then do we not fear a loss of boundary? Where, then, is the center?

We show the need for a center, a place we can be ourselves and at peace in the presence of God, in all our works. We see prayer as being this unifying principle—not as one more demand on an already overburdened life, but as the atmosphere and unity of all the fragments of our life.

The earliest book about prayer was written by Origen, and in it he says something that goes to the heart of our problem: "He prays unceasingly who combines prayer with necessary duties and duties with prayer. Only in this way can we find it practicable to fulfill the commandment to pray always. It consists in regarding the whole of Christian existence as a single great prayer. What we are accustomed to call prayer is only a part of it."

Modern spiritual writer Henri Nouwen expresses this need for finding a center to hold together all of life in prayer, in this way: "We need . . . a way of living in which all we do becomes prayer . . . not just to say prayers but to live a prayerful life . . . anchored in the hub where all the elements of our fragmented life meet like spokes of a wheel."

One way to approach what Nouwen writes about is through a meditative technique that enables us to have this "centeredness," for example by using the Jesus Prayer or some other way of praying. This is a good practice but secondary to the attitude of heart in which prayer can live. And if we do not have that attitude of heart, then there is the risk that every technique will only serve for a short time. We will tire of it.

But look to the example of one man in whose life an attitude of continual prayer to God seems exemplified, who speaks about this clearly and simply: Brother Lawrence, a lay monk who lived in the seventeenth century and who authored a book, *The Practice of the Presence of God*. I recommend this book, which is very short and available online, to everyone.

Brother Lawrence had been deeply troubled for some years by a fear that he would be damned. But he finally decided to set aside the problem, vowing to live the rest of his life trying to love God, knowing that, no matter what followed, it was simply a good thing to do.

Since that moment, he wrote, he "passed his life in perfect liberty and continual joy."

At the same time he related his experience (speaking of himself in the third person), saying that he became convinced of the need of a continual inner conversation with God. "That we ought to speak to God with the greatest simplicity . . . frankly and plainly . . . asking his assistance in our affairs just as they happen. That God never failed to grant it, as he had often experienced."

When there was a failure, he would say to God, "Unless you help me I will never do better, you must hinder my failing, and mend what is amiss." Then after saying this he gave himself no further uneasiness about the failure.

In this way he found a sense of peace that stayed with him even in duties for which he had a natural aversion, giving the example of work in the kitchen or tasks that were hard for him, being lame. But even in these, in committing them from moment to moment to God, he found complete peace and success.

Even though he followed the monastery rule of prayer, "with him the set times of prayer were not different from other times because his greatest business did not divert him from God."

Now, these simple principles of Brother Lawrence will not produce the same effect in any two persons. But they are important to remember and to return to again and again: to be aware of our failures, our limitations, our repeated and useless thoughts, and patterns of doing things; not to be defeated by them but speaking of them again to God, returning to the present moment ready to receive what is here and now. To also from moment to moment bless and thank God for all the little gifts of each moment and of each person we meet, this too makes us free to receive. His simple "practice" shows us how to begin to be free from our self-centeredness, and to open the door to a larger life.

In giving an example of a life in continual conversation with God, we could have the objection—does not this talking with God all the time separate us from others and make ordinary conversation impossible?

But we find it is just the opposite. When we are at rest in God and see others in relation to God, we feel drawn closer to them. This is because we are seeing them, a lit-tle, with God's eyes.

And as we see the world in this way, God's love and acceptance of the other enters us, and makes the other not a stranger but, at a deep level, a friend, or a friend-to-be. We have met the other at a depth where each person begins and ends, and found the origin in God that we have in common, and in which we are destined to a unity, a friendship—*sobornost.*

We know that a circle can have an infinite number of radii moving from the center that become progressively far-ther apart and yet all meet at the center. So it is with us. Each of us in our experience of the journey of life, and in what we suffer and enjoy and discover, moves in a unique direction over space that no one else has traveled. But there remains the center, where, whatever our experience and personality, we are in God and at the same place. So a life that is anchored in prayer, and in the awareness of and reaching out to God, will be very close to every other life.

Mission is a journey together to the center, to Christ. It is a journey of the church and the world together, and in smaller form it is the journey of Christian and non-Christian together.

Within the church it is also not simply an arrival, as if the task of mission were to bring people to church and then close the door with people inside. But it is a journey through the Word of God to its depth in Christ and through sacrament to the Lord, who gives his body and blood to us.

If the fragmented experience characteristic of our time makes us especially aware of our need for inner centeredness, it also shows us that mission is not at all just a formal activity of "convincing" others, but rather it is a call the Lord gives to us to come beyond the forms to the realities. To travel together as communities in Christ, and together also in mission with those who do not yet know Christ.

Is not this journey together exemplified simply and beautifully in John 1:38–39 where inquirers ask Jesus, "Master, where do you dwell?" He replies, "Come and see," and they travel together to his place.

If complexity, hypocrisy, pretending to be what we know we are not, fear, and illusion are all symptoms of the divided state of the world, then it is the opposite that is the nature of this mission impelled by the journey inward to the Lord.

Simplicity. Humility. Genuineness. Reality and peace. These are the characteristics that come from a life anchored in prayer, and they are also the way—and the end—of the missionary journey.

We can find many examples of prayer, conversation with God, and its result in life. We learned of Brother Lawrence's prayer. And we may think of the example of Frere Roger of Taize, who spoke of life as a pilgrimage of trust on earth: continually, from moment to moment, reaching out in trust to God.

And so, as we see each other in Christ, even for a moment, we become aware of this center in each life without exception, even in those who are far from being aware of it. We see how at the end of our journey of mission, all, with all our varied experiences, will be gathered in Christ, and our song will be, as an old writer said, thinking of a circle superimposed with a common center, each unique but all together, a *sobornost,* "a choir of centers."

As we realize how this can be, and must be, perhaps we are freed from fear of the surface divisions and confusions and disorder in the world and in the church because we have discovered—just a little—what the church really is in Christ.

After all the words, what remains for us? Only to find and to enter a moment of friends in union.

Epilogue

Now it is early autumn in Semkhoz. The trees are heavy with apples and the birch trees are tinged with yellow.

In the simple dining room of the retreat house, morning sun streams through the windows. Breakfast is being prepared, plates and trays of food being brought from the kitchen. Before eating we will stand and sing the Lord's Prayer facing the windows and a copy of the icon of the *The Holy Trinity* by Andrey Rublev.

In the icon, one of the Three has set a cup on the table with a gesture of invitation. This side of the table is open.

Beside the icon, there is a small square window full of light and the green of an apple tree.

The images merge, painting and window, and appear as one. *Sobornost* shimmers in the crisp morning air as we, here, are gathered together.

Appendix

bibliographical notes and suggestions for further reading

Part One

1.

Fr. Alexander Men (1935–1990) was an architect of, and guide for, the renewal of Christian faith in Russia. His importance for Russia is clear, but beyond that, his importance for the universal church is coming into view. In any case, as the reader will find, he has been of the greatest importance in my own life, and I find his words to our subject of *sobornost* to be vital and prophetic.

A good starting point for learning more about Fr. Men is the biography *Alexander Men* by Yves Hamant (Redondo Beach, CA: Oakwood, 1995), which is also richly illustrated with photographs that make present the whole time of Russia's turning toward faith.

Early on I cite at some length from Fr. Men's recorded conversations in homes, and these are available in *On Christ and the Church* (Crestwood, NY: St. Vladimir's Seminary Press, 1996).

Beyond these, however, the interested reader might wish to explore an excellent website that makes available a great deal of Fr. Men's writing and some memoirs of him: www.alexandermen.com.

2.

The article "The Difficult Path to Dialogue: On Graham Greene's Monsignor Quixote," as translated by Steven Griffin, originally appeared in *First Hour*, a magazine I edited for some years, and is now on the Alexander Men website (www.alexandermen.com).

3.

Catherine de Hueck Doherty's *Sobornost* (Montreal, Canada: Madonna House, 2000) is a meditation of this theme within a set of three, including *Molchanie* (Silence) and *Pustina* (Hermitage). It is an important work within her spirituality and that of Madonna House, which she founded, and also as the only popular book devoted to the theme of *sobornost*.

4–7.

For the Russian development of *sobornost*, *On Spiritual Unity: A Slavophile Reader* (Hudson, NY: Lindisfarne Books, 1998) provides a good collection of central materials, including "The Church Is One" by Alexei Khomiakov, some writings of Ivan Kireyevsky, and responses from Nikolai Berdyaev and Fr. Pavel Florensky. For those who wish to go further, the two-volume *History of Russian Philosophy* by Zenkovsky (New York: Routledge, Kegan & Paul, 1953) and the single-volume *History of Russian Philosophy* by Nicholas Lossky (London: Henderson & Spalding, 1952) are important and I have used these as well as Georges Florovsky's two-volume *Ways of Russian Theology* (Belmont, MA: Nordland, 1979).

For the general reader I would recommend *The Russian Idea* by Nikolai Berdyaev (Hudson, NY: Lindisfarne, 1992). Also we have used Sergei Bulgakov's *The Orthodox Church* (Crestwood, NY: St. Vladimir's Seminary Press, 1988). But especially let me recommend *Vladimir Soloviev: Russian Mystic*, a very readable, and I think insightful, biography of this most important of nineteenth-century Russian spiritual thinkers by Paul M. Allen (New York: Multimedia, 1978). Soloviev's whole broad-ranging spiritual quest flows from the search for the unity that is *sobornost.*

9.

Nicholas Afanasiev's *The Church of the Holy Spirit* (Notre Dame, IN: Notre Dame University Press, 2007) is an important work for those with an interest in church history. The play "Terror of the Light" by Charles Williams is from his *Collected Plays* (Berkeley, CA: Regent, 2006).

12.

Fr. Lev Gillet's attraction to *sobornost* and concern at seeing it not lived out and realized is noted by his biographer Elisabeth Behr-Sigel, in *Lev Gillet: A Monk of the Eastern Church* (London: Fellowship of Sts. Alban and Sergius, 1999).

Dietrich Bonhoeffer's *Life Together* (San Francisco: HarperSanFrancisco, 1993) is a small treasure that rewards the attention of anyone drawn to or interested in life in community.

13.

On Mother Maria Skobtsova, the biography by Fr. Sergei Hackel, who knew her, is a wonderful book: *Pearl of Great Price* (Crestwood, NY: St. Vladimir's Seminary Press, 1981). More recently, some of her key writings have been collected in the Modern Spiritual Masters series from Orbis Books as *Essential Writings*, trans. Richard Pevear and Larissa Volokhonsky (Maryknoll, NY: Orbis, 2003). Mother Maria's quoted statement is taken from "The Mysticism of Human Communio," page 79.

On Charles Williams's doctrine of exchanged love I used his *Essential Writings in Spirituality and Theology* (Cambridge, MA: Cowley, 1993), particularly the essay "The Way of Exchange." I would also like to mention a perhaps unusual, but I think interesting, work, the graphic novel *Heaven's War* by Micah Harris (Berkeley, CA: Image Comics, 2004), which among other things interprets the doctrine of exchange as a key to understanding Williams own life.

15.

On friendship as *sobornost* I have particularly used and commend to the reader Letter 11 of *The Pillar and Ground of Truth: An Essay in Orthodox Theodicy in Twelve Letters* by Pavel

Florensky. (Princeton, NJ: Princeton University Press, 1997). I have drawn Antoine Arjakowsky's thoughts on "ecumenism based on friendship" from personal conversation, but I recommend his *Church, Culture and Identity* (Lviv, Ukraine: Catholic University Press, 2007).

16.

Fr. Alexander Men's "Two Understandings of Christianity" is a brief essay of the greatest importance in the meditation of *sobornost*, of the unity of diverse people in love. It is at the website cited above, www.alexandermen.com, and can also be found in the collection of his work, unfortunately now out of print, *Christianity for the XXIst Century* (New York: Continuum, 1996).

18.

Thomas Merton's story of the monks escaping with the monastery goods on the back of yaks is from his last talk given in Bangkok and included in his *Asian Journal* (New York: New Directions, 1975).

Part Two

From Teilhard I refer in particular to *The Divine Milieu* (New York: Perennial, 2001). The expression "the ages of the spiritual life" resonates to the book of that name by Pavel Evdokimov (Crestwood, NY: St. Vladimir's Seminary Press, 1998) in which also his development of the idea of "interior monasticism" is of particular importance. *The Philokalia* (New York: Faber & Faber, 1998) has a great deal to say on watchfulness as understood by a broad spectrum of writers of various streams in the Eastern tradition, especially in volume 4.

The quotation from Fr. Serge Bulgakov in section 5 is found in his autobiographical notes included in the *Bulgakov Anthology* (London: SPCK, 1976). In the same section I refer to another wonderful and deeply personal work, the *Journals of Father Alexander Schmemann* (Crestwood, NY: St. Vladimir's Seminary Press, 2003).

Part Three

1.

On the scientific side of complementarity, Niels Bohr is most important and a good, brief account of his thought is given in Ruth Moore's *Niels Bohr: The Man, His Science, and the World They Changed* (Cambridge, MA: MIT Press, 1985), a very readable biography.

For a general introduction to quantum problematics, there are many popular books, but I should like to suggest *Mr. Tompkins in Wonderland* by George Gamow (Cambridge, UK: The University Press, 1940) as an entertaining book, sound in its science, that will remain in your mind after much else is forgotten.

Like Mr. Tompkins, perhaps a bit outside the box, I would suggest the play *Copenhagen* by Peter Michael Frayn as giving both a sense of what Bohr and the others were up to and also, and with real depth, a sense of how several variously limited men and women can complete each other's limitations in a human complementarity parallel to that within the atom.

2.

On the side of Christian reflection on complementarity, I would recommend in particular Nicholas da Cusa's *Vision of God*, available within the Paulist Press Classics of Western Spirituality volume of his work published in 1997, and separately, and with an introduction by Evelyn Underhill, from Cosimo in 2007.

Of recent philosophers, the work of Simeon Frank, the great philosopher of the Russian emigration, is most grounded in complementarity. He develops this with great depth in his work *The Unknowable* (Athens, OH: Ohio University, 1983).

The quotations from Chico Martin and Andrey Cherniak are from personal correspondence.

Fr. Alexander Men's story of the young man vacillating between the Baptist and Orthodox churches is found in Yves Hamant's biography cited earlier.

Part Four

Origen's "On Prayer" is included in *Alexandrian Christianity*, The Library of Christian Classics (London: SCM Press, 1954). Of Henri Nouwen I would commend especially *The Heart of Henri Nouwen* (New York: Crossroad, 2003).

The Practice of the Presence of God of Brother Lawrence is as essential as any book I know on the subject of prayer. It is available in many editions, and even is fully available online, for example at: http://www.practicegodspresence.com/brotherlawrence/practicegodspresence09.html.

fiction and poetry; and the Active Prayer Series that brings creativity and liveliness to any life of prayer.

Recordings

From Gregorian chant to contemporary American choral works, our music recordings celebrate sacred choral music through the centuries. Paraclete distributes the recordings of the internationally acclaimed choir Gloriæ Dei Cantores, praised for their "rapt and fathomless spiritual intensity" by *American Record Guide*, and the Gloriæ Dei Cantores Schola, which specializes in the study and performance of Gregorian chant. Paraclete is also the exclusive North American distributor of the recordings of the Monastic Choir of St. Peter's Abbey in Solesmes, France, long considered to be a leading authority on Gregorian chant.

DVDs

Our DVDs offer spiritual help, healing, and biblical guidance for life issues: grief and loss, marriage, forgiveness, anger management, facing death, and spiritual formation.

Learn more about us at our website:
www.paracletepress.com, or call us toll-free
at 1-800-451-5006.

about Paraclete Press

Who We Are

Paraclete Press is a publisher of books, recordings, and DVDs on Christian spirituality. Our publishing represents a full expression of Christian belief and practice—from Catholic to Evangelical, from Protestant to Orthodox.

We are the publishing arm of the Community of Jesus, an ecumenical monastic community in the Benedictine tradition. As such, we are uniquely positioned in the marketplace without connection to a large corporation and with informal relationships to many branches and denominations of faith.

What We Are Doing
Books

Paraclete publishes books that show the richness and depth of what it means to be Christian. Although Benedictine spirituality is at the heart of all that we do, we publish books that reflect the Christian experience across many cultures, time periods, and houses of worship. We publish books that nourish the vibrant life of the church and its people—books about spiritual practice, formation, history, ideas, and customs.

We have several different series, including the best-selling Paraclete Essentials and Paraclete Giants series of classic texts in contemporary English; A Voice from the Monastery—men and women monastics writing about living a spiritual life today; award-winning literary faith